►► *FastForward*™

with
Jeff
mmer

Rhythm Riffs
ForKeyboard

Riffs, Licks ... ...ay!
MW00850916

Wise Publications
London / New York / Sydney / Paris / Copenhagen / Madrid

Exclusive Distributors:
Music Sales Limited
8/9 Frith Street, London W1V 5TZ, England.
Music Sales Pty Limited
120 Rothschild Avenue, Rosebery, NSW 2018, Australia.
Music Sales Corporation
257 Park Avenue South, New York, NY10010,
United States of America.

Order No. AM92436
ISBN 0-7119-4512-8
This book © Copyright 1997 by Wise Publications.

Unauthorised reproduction of any part of this
publication by any means including photocopying is
an infringement of copyright.

Book design by Michael Bell Design.
Edited and arranged by Jeff Hammer.
Music processed by Interactive Music Sciences Limited.
Cover photography by George Taylor.
Cover instrument kindly loaned by Rose Morris Limited.
Text photographs courtesy of
London Features International and Barry Plummer.
Printed and bound in the United Kingdom.

Your Guarantee of Quality:
As publishers, we strive to produce every book to
the highest commercial standards.
The music has been freshly engraved and the book has
been carefully designed to minimise awkward page turns
and to make playing from it a real pleasure.
Particular care has been given to specifying acid-free,
neutral-sized paper made from pulps which have not
been elemental chlorine bleached.
This pulp is from farmed sustainable forests and
was produced with special regard for the environment.
Throughout, the printing and binding have
been planned to ensure a sturdy, attractive publication
which should give years of enjoyment.
If your copy fails to meet our high standards, please
inform us and we will gladly replace it.

Music Sales' complete catalogue describes
thousands of titles and is available in full colour sections
by subject, direct from Music Sales Limited.
Please state your areas of interest and send a cheque/postal
order for £1.50 for postage to: Music Sales Limited,
Newmarket Road, Bury St. Edmunds, Suffolk IP33 3YB.

Visit the Internet Music Shop at
http://www.musicsales.co.uk

Introduction

Hello, and welcome to ▶▶**Fast**_Forward_ Congratulations on purchasing a product that will improve your playing and provide you with hours of pleasure. All the music in this book has been specially created by professional musicians to give you maximum value and enjoyability.

If you already know how to 'drive' your instrument but you'd like to do a little customising, you've pulled in at the right place. We'll put you on the fast track to playing the kinds of riffs and patterns that today's professionals rely on.

We'll provide you with a vocabulary of riffs that you can apply in a wide variety of musical situations, with a special emphasis on giving you the techniques that will help you in a band situation. That's why every music example in this book comes with a full-band audio track so that you get your chance to join in. All players and all bands get their sounds and styles by drawing on the same basic building blocks. With ▶▶**Fast**_Forward_ you'll quickly learn these, and then be ready to use them to create your own style.

Rhythm Riffs For Keyboard

So you've got the keyboard and plenty of sounds - piano, electric piano, organ, clavinet. The drummer, the bassist and the guitarist are ready, and you are about to start the first song. You know the chords - it opens on G - but here the problem starts: 'What do I actually play?'

Being a rock keyboard player involves playing to the rhythm set by the drums, fitting in with the bass guitar part, and complementing the rhythms and lead lines of the guitars. Sound complicated? Well, the more you play your keyboard, the more you will begin to understand the options offered by the various styles of keyboard playing and the various sounds available.

The idea behind this book is not to set out fixed formulas but to suggest a range of starting points. Practise them, experiment with them and, most importantly, don't be afraid to try your own ideas. Remember, there are no rules. You will be surprised just how quickly your own repertoire of riffs will develop.

▶▶ *RAY MANZAREK*

Riff No.1
Piano Style

Playing keyboards in a *rock style* is very different from the solo keyboard approach which is based around the right hand playing the melody with an accompaniment in the left hand.

In a rock band the melody will be taken by the vocalist or soloing instrument and this means the other instruments must find parts to fit around that... riffs. These riffs will form the backbone of a song arrangement – sometimes all the instruments will play the same riff, other times the arrangement will be built around different riffs that lock together to form a foundation for the song, e.g. bass guitar pumping on the root notes, a jangly rhythm guitar part, stabs on the sax... anything missing? Yes, a solid keyboard riff holding it all together.

Anyway, enough chat... let's get on with it. Select a piano sound and try this one-bar riff.

This is a solid riff that will work over both slow and fast rock tempos and can be repeated depending on the number of bars you have to fill. Notice how the last two beats of each bar, where nothing is played, allow space for the other instruments to fit in their riff.

Tip: Sometimes the notes you *don't* play will contribute more to a part of the arrangement than the notes you do! Graduates of the 'Less Is More' school of playing tend to number far fewer than those from the school of 'Why Play One Note When Six Will Do?'. A trip to your local rehearsal studio will illustrate this point!

When you feel comfortable with this shape, try moving from one chord to another...

...and then begin to link-up a whole progression
of chords...

TRACK 3

Variations

To add some variation and a slightly *bluesy*
feel, try slipping between the minor and major
3rd in the right hand.

Adding in the 7th will also add some variation...

...and is an ideal link to the next chord as you begin to use this riff in a chord progression.

TRACK 6

Adding a left-hand *link* over the last two beats of the bar also gives a *bluesy* feel and will help to add some variation to the rhythmic structure of this riff.

TRACK 7

Tip: By *occasionally* using a variation you will avoid the riff becoming monotonous – over-use of variations will make the keyboard part seem *cluttered*. Think about it in terms of *adding colour* as you play, don't work to a system as this will become monotonous yet again!

The final variation we're going to look at in this chapter is playing the riff using a PUSH.

Instead of the riff being played *on* the first beat of the bar, it can be *pushed* a quarter beat earlier.

TRACK 8

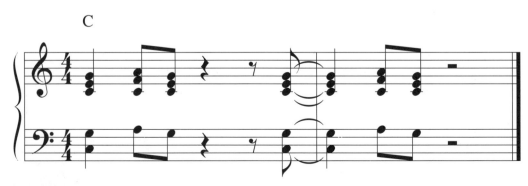

Try playing through this chord progression
which now has a *push* on alternate bars – this will
help you appreciate the difference in feel.

 TRACK 9

Tip: Unlike the other variations which only
affect the keyboard part, using a *push* will involve
the rest of the musicians as you will need to play
any *pushes* together. Remember the golden rule –
don't overdo it!

Think in terms of using a *push* for the first
chord of a chorus... or the beginning of a verse...
or as a feature in a bridge section.

It's better to have one *push* that all the band
play, than twelve *pushes* that some of you play...
at different times. You want people to tap their
feet to your music, not trip over to it!

▶▶ *ELTON JOHN*
"Every day I used to come home from school and play until somebody was able to make me stop. Eventually my mother and father became nervous wrecks and we had complaints from the neighbours."

Riff No. 2
Two-Bar Piano Riff

Select a piano sound and try this two-bar riff.

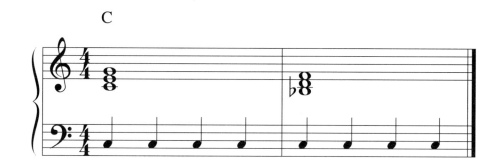

This riff also leaves plenty of space for the other instruments and by moving away from the notes of the basic C chord (C-E-G) provides greater scope for the melody or a solo.

Tip: The chord in the second bar can be described in two ways – C11 or B=flat over C (B♭/C); both are correct. As a general rule, if you want to present yourself as a serious, heavily jazz-influenced musician call it C11, but if you're dealing with rock musicians... stick to B♭ over C!

Now try moving the riff to another chord...

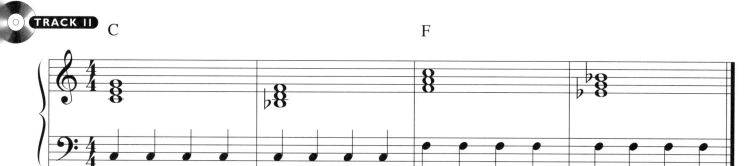

Tip: By using a different inversion of the F chord (i.e. the same notes but played in a different order) the riff becomes slightly easier to play as the right hand doesn't have to jump around so much...

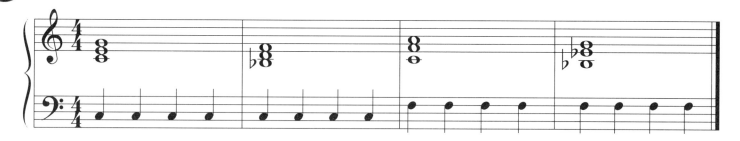

Compare the sound of the following example built around a progression of C-F-D-G using tonic chords (i.e. root note at the bottom of each chord)...

TRACK 13

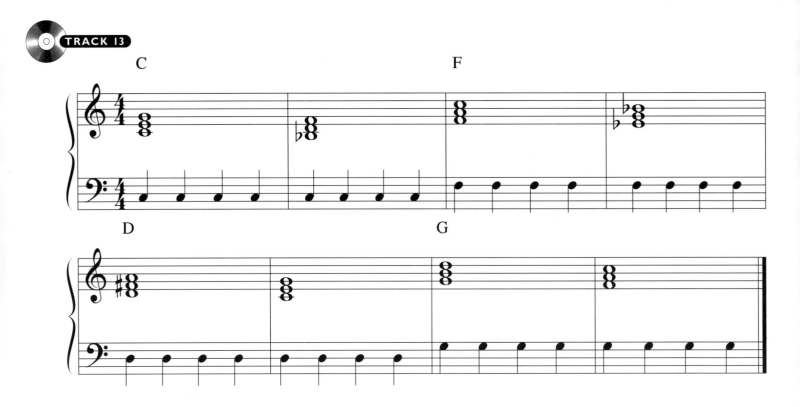

...with this example using 2nd inversion chords for F and G. Notice how this allows your right hand to play the progression with minimal hand movement.

TRACK 14

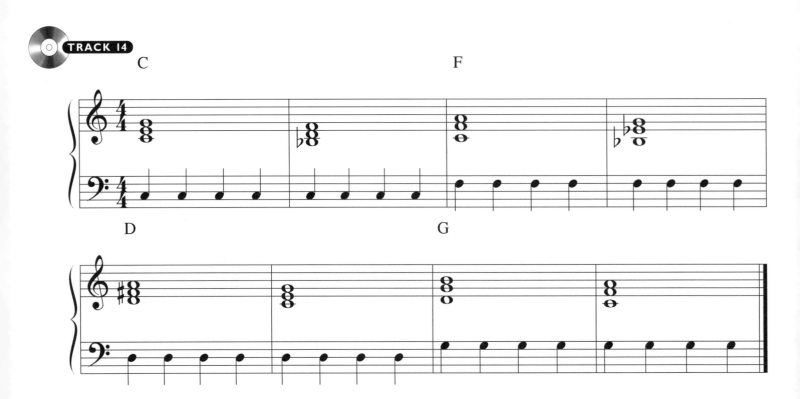

Tip: Using the tonic chords tends to underline the movement of the chord progression giving a more *up* feel (good for a chorus?), whereas the inversions give a more *understated* sound to the progression (better for a verse or bridge?)... but experiment with them and see what your ears tell you!

Having seen the use of chord inversions to add variation to this riff, we can take this even further by adding other chord inversions into each bar.

The following version of the riff illustrates this over four bars...

TRACK 15

...but remember, this is just to add variation so don't lose sight of the original riff by becoming over-complicated.

The *push* feel, as mentioned on page 8, will also be effective with this riff...

TRACK 16

At first, playing a push feel can often be rather jerky and snatched – play round the following chords so that each push becomes relaxed and smooth.

TRACK 17

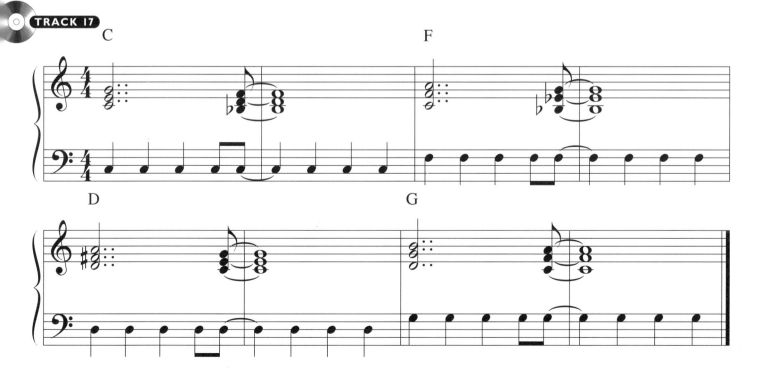

▶▶ *JERRY LEE LEWIS*

Riff No. 3
Two-Bar Piano Riff

Select a piano sound and try this two-bar riff.

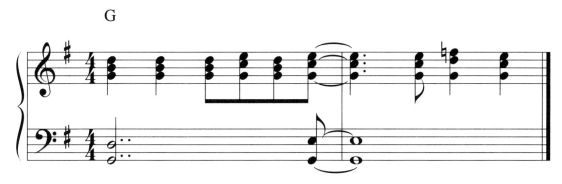

This is a fuller riff that fits well with faster rock tempos and a straight bass guitar feel of *fours* (crotchet beats) or *eights* (quaver beats). Keep going round the two-bar pattern until playing this slightly more complex keyboard part feels natural to you.

Then try moving the riff from G to C...

...and when you're on top of that, move on to
this four-chord progression.

Tip: *Busier* riffs like this one are obviously
more distinctive and, therefore, more thought
needs to go into their use, so... would it be
a good *hook* for the intro and link sections?...
is it right for the verse or bridge?... or would
it lift the chorus?

Over-use will lessen the impact – familiarity
breeds contempt!

Variations

The *bluesy* idea of slipping the thirds from
minor to major will work well with this riff...

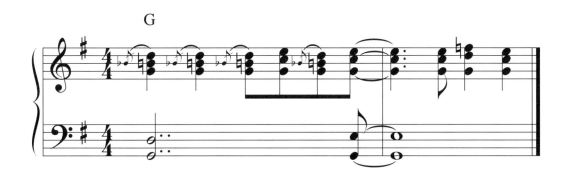

Having already seen that a full riff like this one
needs to be used selectively, other variations will
need to be found that maintain some continuity
whilst moving more into the background.

This example provides variation by stripping
out some parts of the riff...

Tip: If you want to have dynamics in your
playing, you need to create contrasts – you can
only have highs if there have been some

lows so... strip it down to the bare minimum,
one chord per bar...

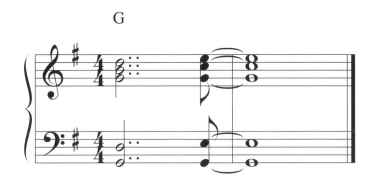

...maybe even play the right hand an
octave lower.

...and feel the arrangement shift up a gear when
the riff comes steaming back in!!

▶▶ *KEITH EMERSON*

Riff No. 4
Piano Style With Straight Eights

Select a piano sound and try this riff.

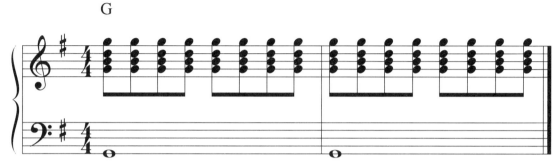

This style of playing is very much a feature of rock piano playing and is based on a constant eights feel (quaver beats) throughout the bar. Although the rhythm part is fixed, the actual chords used can be flexible.

The starting point is with tonic chords (i.e. root note at the bottom of the chord) – try moving from G to C...

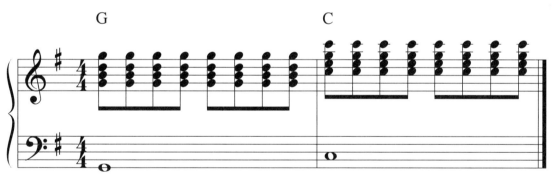

...another way of playing this is to go from the tonic chord of G to the second inversion of C...

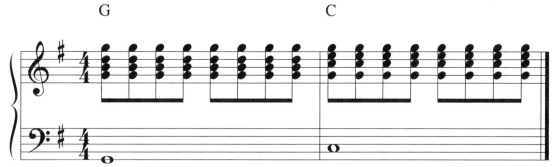

...notice how the chords seem to blend together more and it's easier to play as only two fingers need to move!

Tip: This riff is great for creating a feeling of intensity and excitement... try it out in the upper octaves of the piano.

Accurate and precise playing, however, is very important... it might LOOK great to leap off the stool, sending it flying backwards as you crash

into the eights feel in the final chorus, but... if it SOUNDS like you're wearing boxing gloves and a blindfold it tends to lessen the impact!

There are no set rules for deciding which chord inversions to use. Tonic chords tend to stress the movement within a chord progression more than inversions.

The following is a good example of this...

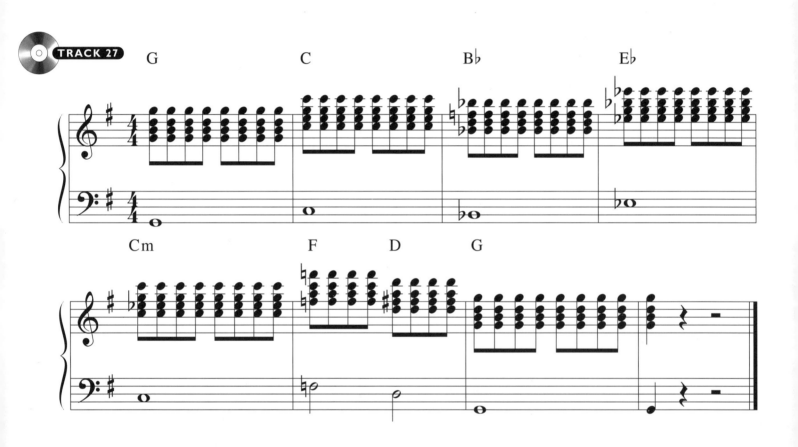

By using other inversions the same chord progressions can be played using just one octave in the right hand.

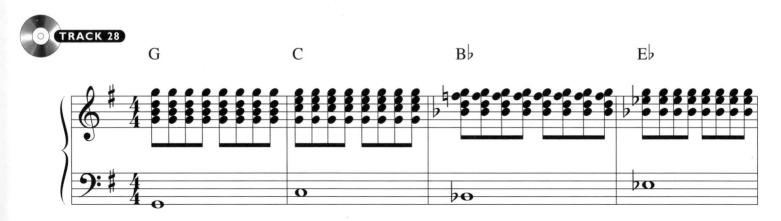

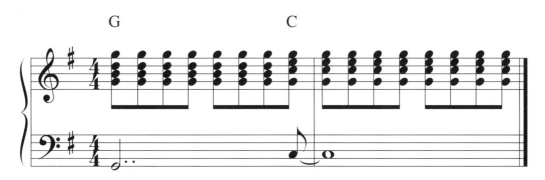

Notice how this example also keeps a G on the top of every chord – this keeps up the intensity and links the chord progression to the basic key signature.

If you want to know whether this will work with a chord progression that you are working with, just try it and your ear will tell you the answer!

A *push* can also be used effectively with this riff and will involve changing the chord one quaver beat earlier.

TRACK 29

Tip: It might appear that 'just playing eights' must be easy - but staying in TIME and in TUNE requires accurate playing so it is advisable to use it at first in short bursts... desperately clutching your cramp-ridden wrist in the middle of a song is likely to be a distraction to those around you!

Final tip: If the thought crosses your mind to 'do a Jerry Lee Lewis' and play this riff with your elbows, knees or feet... first, make sure it's not your keyboard!!

▶▶ LITTLE RICHARD

Riff No. 5
Clavinet Style

In this chapter we're going to look at another keyboard sound – clavinet. The tone of the clavinet is hard and punchy, combining thick, fat sounds in the lower octaves with bright, cutting upper octaves.

When using the clavinet sound think percussively – the tonal quality of the notes played will alter depending on the velocity (i.e. how hard you play them!) which gives instant dynamics and colour at your finger-tips.

Select a clavinet sound and then try the right-hand part of this riff...

The left hand is based on the same rhythmic construction as the right hand but moves like a bass guitar line...

When you feel comfortable playing each of these parts, try playing them together.

Tip: Experiment with the percussive qualities of the clavinet sound... emphasise different parts of the riff – lay into those left-hand notes, punch out the right hand and... get funky!

As the left-hand part of the riff is so distinctive it is likely that you will continue it through a chord progression – this will need some practise especially as other instruments might double the line with you (play the same part), making accurate playing a necessity.

This progression moves through C-F-C-G-F-C; pay particular attention to the links before each new chord...

 TRACK 33

As we introduce the right-hand part we can take two different approaches.

The first is to move the right-hand part with each new chord...

 TRACK 34

This gives emphasis to the movement within the chord progression and tends to make more of a feature of the actual right-hand part.

The other approach is to keep the right-hand part the same and just move the left hand through the chord progression.

 TRACK 35

This makes the progression *blend* more and understates the right-hand part.

Tip: You could switch to the above example during another instrument's solo.

▶▶ *TOM WAITS*
"I can remember working in a restaurant and hearing music come out of the jukebox and wondering how to get from where I was, in my apron and paper hat, through all the convoluted stuff that takes you to where you're coming out of the jukebox."

Variations

Because this clavinet riff is contributing to the rhythm as well as the tonality of the arrangement, the scope for variation is very wide...

Try playing just the first half of the right-hand part...

...switch it around and play only the second half.

Play the right-hand an octave lower...
Double the left-hand part with the right hand...

Tip: Experiment with the percussive potential of this sound... think of a percussionist playing

congas and use a similar style to improvise around this riff on your keyboard... it might be an idea to plug in your headphones!!

▶▶ *KATE BUSH*

Riff No. 6
Clavinet Style With Left-Hand Emphasis

The riff in this chapter also features the clavinet but the emphasis is on the left hand.

The lower octaves of a clavinet produce a sound that is *thick* and *fat*, especially when the keys are played with a lot of *attack*.

Use the following example to master playing the notes of the riff but also to get used to maintaining a constant *rolling* feel, especially as you jump the octave down to the first beat of each bar.

TRACK 38

Once the riff has started to *roll* effortlessly move on to the next example which introduces a second chord...

TRACK 39

The *jump* down to the first note of each bar is the tricky part of this riff so be honest with yourself as you work through the following chord progression – each first beat should be just as *smooth* as the rest of the bar...

Tip: Use the fingering suggested in the following example – working on this now will pay off later.

Variations

Introducing an element of variation will prevent the sound of the riff becoming monotonous, and a slight change to the notes or the *groove* is the best approach so the feel of the riff remains solid.

The following variation adds a semi-quaver to the 3rd beat of bar 2 which slightly changes the *groove*...

 TRACK 41

...and as you move to a second chord make sure that the riff and the variation have the same *rolling* feel...

Use this chord progression as an exercise in
switching from riff to variation...

TRACK 43

Tip: Obviously this example *over-plays*
the variation, so now try looping round the
progression adding the variation occasionally –

think in terms of adding *colour* to the groove,
not playing to a formula!

The next variation introduces a *stop* to the riff and will therefore have quite a marked influence on the *groove*.

For now, use this example to get used to both the *stop* and the *start* on the first beat of the following bar...

TRACK 44

...now move to the second chord...

TRACK 45

...and then try the progression, particularly concentrating on keeping a smooth *feel* after each *stop*.

Tip: The *stops* in this last variation provide an ideal moment to feature an instrumental *fill* – a jangling guitar, a bass lick, a drum fill, a keyboard run.

It's a chance to add some musical highlights, not to compete over *who can get the most notes into a 1¾ beat-break!!*

As this is a *busy* left-hand riff, the right hand will be most effective if it sticks to adding occasional chords.

The chords featured here are minor 9ths and are played at the first inversion... play through them to get used to their sound and shape.

 TRACK 47

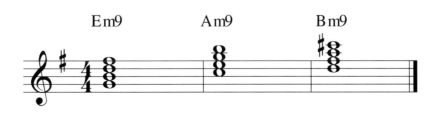

▶▶ JOOLS HOLLAND
"Making the decision to become a musician wasn't so much an identity crisis as a series of revelations."

Now try adding one right-hand chord to
every alternate riff...

TRACK 48

...and then move to the second chord...

TRACK 49

...and now through the chord progression remembering to ensure that there is no glitch in the feel as you add each chord or as you begin to introduce any of the previous left-hand variations.

Riff No. 7
Organ Style

Another classic keyboard sound is the organ – Hammond with swirling Leslie speakers, Farfisa, Vox Continental *etc*... each with their own distinctive sound and all of which have featured on record and on stage since the 60s.

Modern keyboards tend to feature a selection of organ sounds, the one you select will depend on the nature of the song and the character of the part you are going to play.

An up-tempo lighter rock song might suit a brighter *cheesy* Vox-type sound, whereas a harder rock feel would probably need a thick, *growling* Hammond-type sound. But try them all out... the decision is yours!

Select an organ sound and have a look at this riff...

TRACK 51

...you will notice it doesn't start on the first beat of a bar. A one-bar count-in is 1-AND-2-AND-3-AND-4-AND so this

riff starts on the AND after 3. Now give yourself a count and try playing the riff...

TRACK 52

Playing part of the riff prior to the 1st beat of the bar makes a chord progression seem less *square* i.e. the chord changes don't *always* happen on the first beat of a bar.

This will feel more natural as you put the riff into a longer chord progression. Try moving through these chords C-F-D-G.

TRACK 53

Tip: If your keyboard has a modulation wheel use it to add a vibrato/Leslie speaker effect – be careful not to push the wheel too far... moving from *swirling Leslie sound* to *buzzing*

Martian bagpipes is all too easily done! You might also be able to assign modulation to the after-touch of your keyboard, allowing you to create a similar effect by note pressure.

Variations

Slipping in the occasional semitone note will give more of a 'soul' feel...

TRACK 54

Rather than thinking of this as a set variation, the best approach is to punctuate the riff with these *semitone slips* which will add *feel* to your playing.

A stripped-down, more solid variation of the riff will help to add dynamics to the keyboard part...

TRACK 55

As you move to another chord, notice how
the *character* of the original riff is maintained...

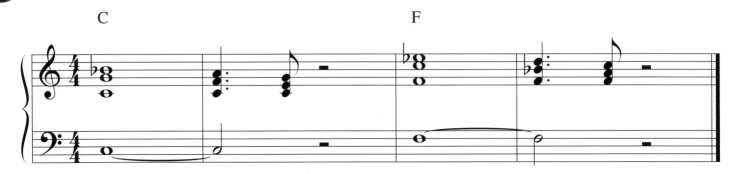

...which means that this variation would be
ideal to play whilst another instrument solos,

or even for a verse or bridge section so that the
main riff is used for a chorus or intro *hook*...

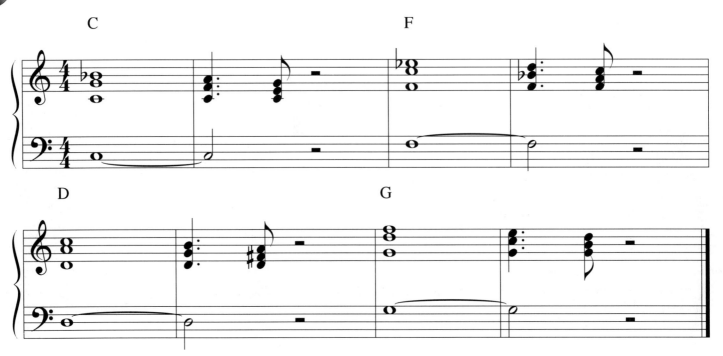

This variation could also feature the *soul* notes
of example 54 on page 32... it might be more
basic than the original riff but it can still groove!

▶▶ *JOE JACKSON*

Riff No. 8
Organ Style With Pad And Lead

Many of the larger classic organs feature a double manual, i.e. two keyboards, which allows the left hand to provide a sustained *pad* using a more mellow setting, while the right hand provides the brighter sounding *lead*.

The riff in this chapter adopts the *double manual* style – block chords in the left hand

with a right-hand lead and can be played without the expense of a second keyboard!

Select a full, sustained organ sound and try this two-bar riff...

TRACK 58

Keep the left-hand chords as *smooth* as possible – (remember the *pad* on the lower organ manual) – whereas the right hand can use a light percussive style attempting to simulate the *click* of an organ.

Work on that as you link the riff to a second chord...

TRACK 59

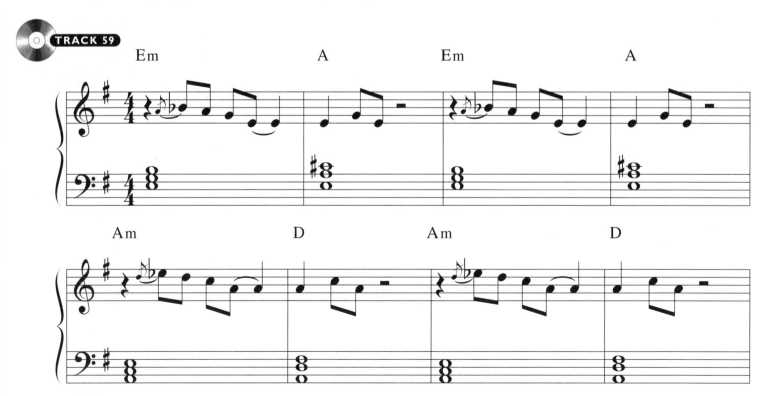

...and then practise maintaining that feel through
a progression of chords...

TRACK 60

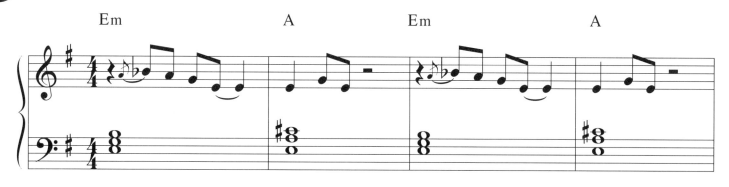

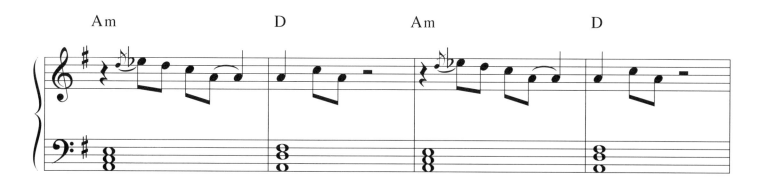

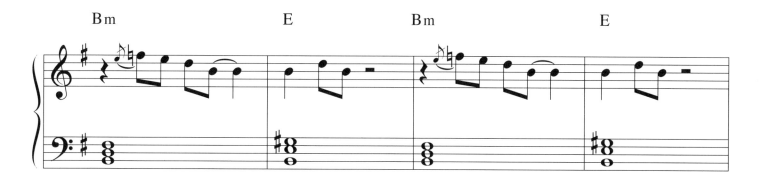

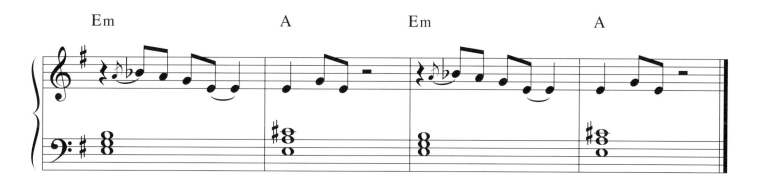

Variations

Moving the opening right-hand note from
a flattened 5th, as in the original riff, to a 5th
changes the character of the sound quite
dramatically – moving away from the *bluesy*
flattened 5th to a soulful *minor* 5th.

Compare this variation to the previous riff...

TRACK 61

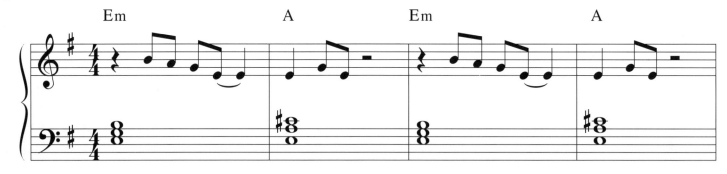

▶▶ **GREGG ALLMAN**
"Before I got into rock 'n' roll, I was going to be a dentist."

...and this example will show how the
semitone change has influenced the other
chords in the progression...

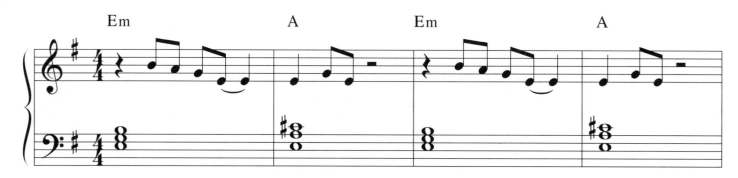

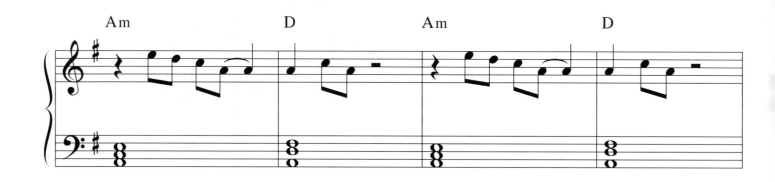

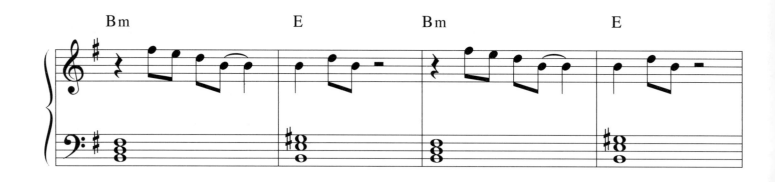

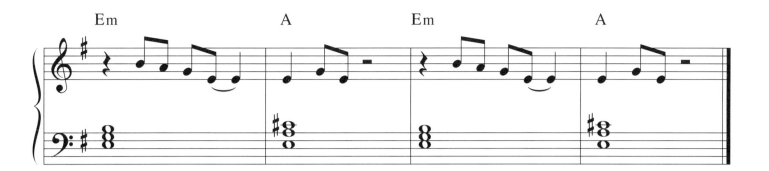

Tip: Decide between the *blues* or *soul* feel and then use an occasional variation – overdoing it will cause confusion and your chosen *mood* will be lost.

To add to the *bluesy* feel of the riff, a *slip* can be added which emphasises the flattened 5th.

Tip: To make the *slip* sound like a guitar *bending* a note, the two keys can be played virtually together with the *slipped* note being released quickly whilst the flattened 5th plays for a full quaver beat.

Use this chord progression to practise making the *slip* sound as much like a *bend* as possible...

TRACK 64

The next variation gives some colour to the
second part of the riff by adding a run into the
second chord ...

Although this variation basically replaces a quaver with two semi-quavers, there is the danger of the riff sounding *wooden* if the performance is not *smooth*, so use the next example to ensure that the *feel* remains steady as you move through the chords.

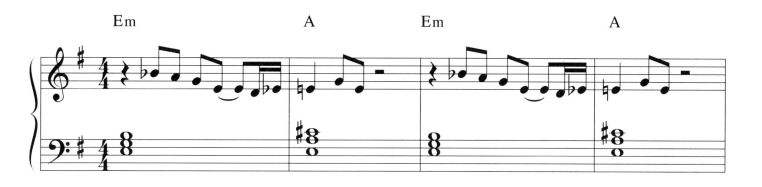

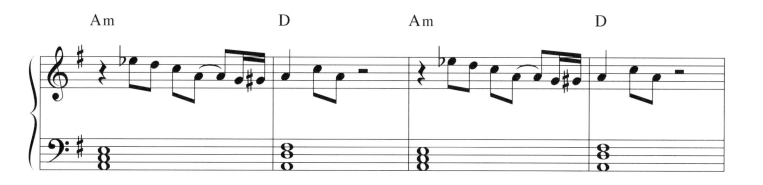

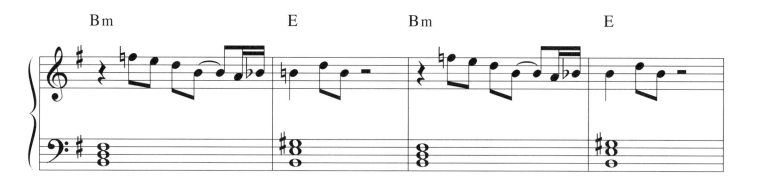

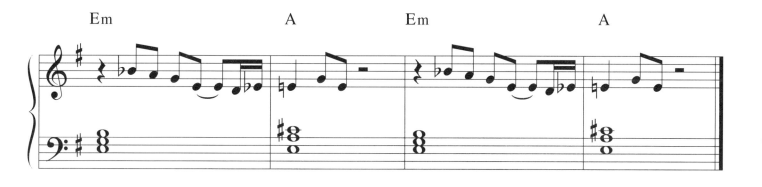

There is also scope for varying the left-hand chords – adding the 7th to the opening minor chord adds some extra character to the sound.

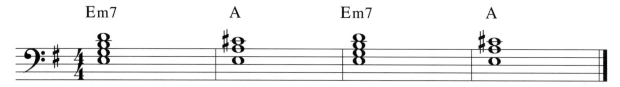

The 7th can be added to the chords in our progression and these are scored out here so that they can be practised by the left hand before adding the right-hand lead-line.

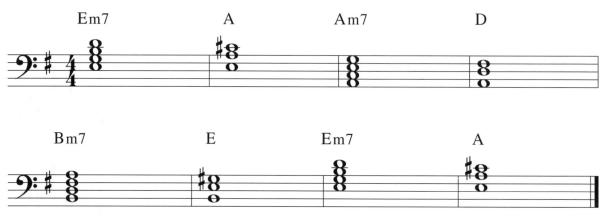

As a final variation both hands can play the block chords, a technique which is useful for building a riff to a climax. With a double-manual organ the sound of each keyboard would blend to create a powerful *wall* of chords, but it can still be effective with a single-manual keyboard.

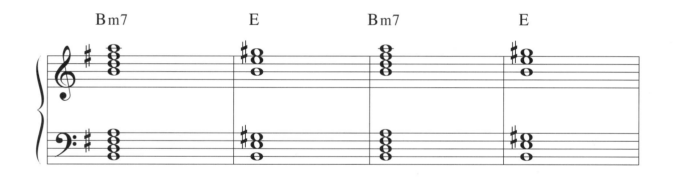

▶▶ *PHIL COLLINS*
"I always imagined myself up on stage when I played, and I always thought of myself as doing this for a living, and not to have to do anything else. This is what I wanted to do."

Riff No. 9
Electric Piano Style

The final keyboard sound we're going to use
is the electric piano – the two classic instruments
in this area are the Fender Rhodes and the
Wurlitzer electric piano, both of which use
vibrating metal bars, rather than strings, to
produce their sound.

Most keyboards feature at least one or two
electric piano presets – the range usually being
from the rich, fuller, more sustained sounds,
to bright, bell-like ones.

The riff in this chapter will work best with
a rich, sustaining electric piano sound (Fender
Rhodes) played over a slower rock tempo using
a triplet feel.

Select an electric piano sound and play this
two-bar riff...

Try to ensure that you sustain the riff right
to the end of the second bar – using the sustain
pedal will allow you to do this and get your

fingers ready for the next chord. Work on
this by moving from Em to Am...

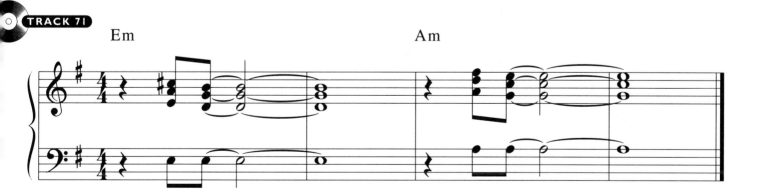

By now you will appreciate the *moody* nature
of this riff and the difference created by a triplet
rhythm part.

Play through this progression and avoid being
too *wooden* as you play each chord... keep it *nice*
and *loose!*

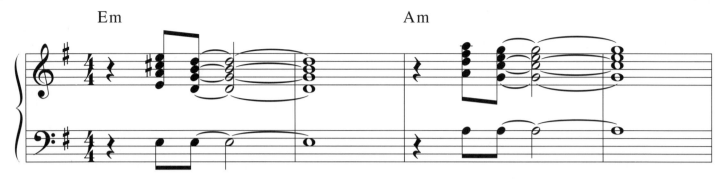

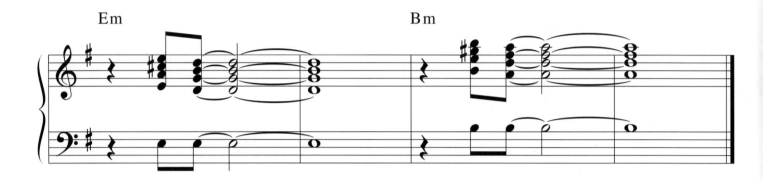

Tip: Adding *chorus* will fatten up the electric
piano sound, and experimenting with your
vibrato settings creates a more authentic stereo
electric piano sound – try a deep, slow vibrato.

Using stereo headphones will help you hear
at once the difference that *chorus* and *tremolo* can
make.

▶▶ *FREDDIE MERCURY*
"I write commercial love songs because basically what I feel very strongly about is love and emotion."

Variations

Making the right hand into full octave chords
gives the riff another colour which you could put
into your part occasionally...

 TRACK 73

You will also need to be comfortable with this
variation using different chords, so work with
this progression until it begins to feel natural...

 TRACK 74

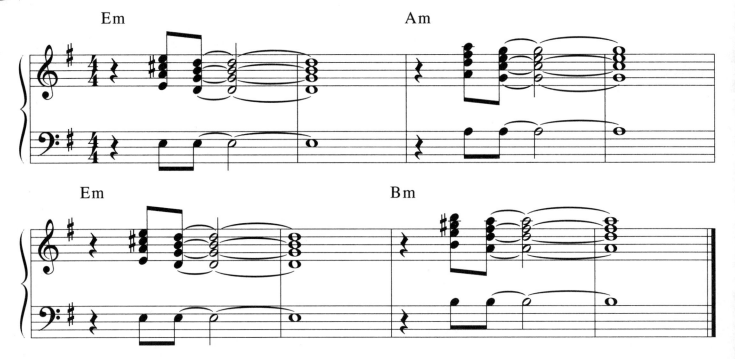

Part of the character of this riff and the mood created by the triplet feel is the sense of space. There is obviously scope to embellish the riff but be careful not to take this too far and fill the spaces with *clutter*... the trick is to just add the occasional *lick*...

TRACK 75

Using the occasional blue note will fit well with the mood of this riff...

TRACK 76

...and there is still scope for variation even if you add a lick only to the last beat of the second bar...

TRACK 77

Tip: The same *'keep it sparse'* rule applies to the other instruments as well – there is no point in your leaving space if someone else comes along and fills it up!

▶▶ *TORI AMOS*
    "Who needs a rhythm section when you have a left hand like hers?" – The Guardian

►► *FastForward*™
Guide To Keyboard

Sitting Correctly

It is important to sit correctly at the keyboard.
The more comfortable you are, the easier it is
to play.

Sit facing the middle of the instrument, with
your feet opposite the pedals. Sit upright with as
straight a back as possible without being stiff.
Your seat should be high enough to allow your arms
to be level with the keyboard, or slightly sloping
down towards it.

The Five Finger Playing Position

With the tips of your fingers, cover five adjacent
white notes in each hand. This is the normal five
finger playing position. It is also the hand's most
relaxed state.

Always return to this position when you have
been playing on other parts of the keyboard.
Like a good squash or tennis player always
occupying the centre of the court, this is the best
'alert' position for keyboard players.

The Hand Position

Support your hands from the wrists, which should
be in a flat position. If you bend your wrists too
much as you play, you will soon experience muscle
fatigue.

Curve your fingers slightly as if you are gently
holding an imaginary ball. Don't extend your fingers
into the keyboard; allow the natural position of
your hand to determine which part of the key you
depress with the tip of your finger.

The Piano Keyboard

There are only seven letter names used in music: A B C D E F G

These seven letter names repeat over and over again on the keyboard. The black keys are arranged in groups of twos and threes.

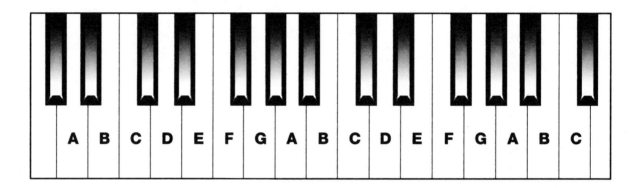

How To Learn The White Keys: C D & E
Use the black keys to locate the white keys.
For example, 'D' lies between two black keys.

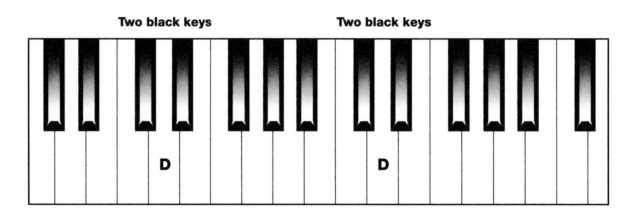

To the left of D lies C. To the right of D lies E.

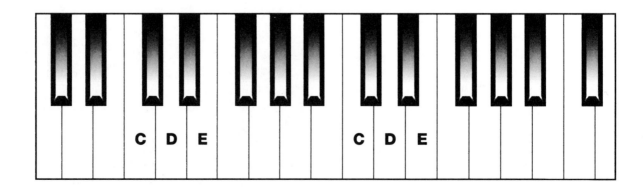

How To Learn The White Keys: F G A & B

Use the groups of three black keys to locate
F, G, A & B (the remaining four letters of the musical
alphabet):

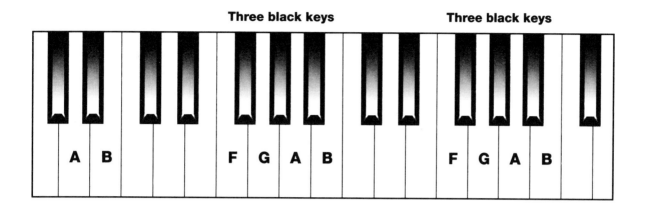

Find all the F's, G's, A's & B's on your piano.
Play each note in turn and name it.

You now know all the white notes and their names.

An Important Note: Middle C

One of the most important notes on the piano
is Middle C. This is the C nearest the middle of
the instrument, directly opposite the manufacturer's
name, as you sit at the piano.

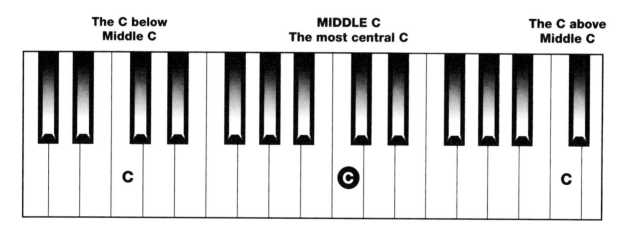

Look at the illustration above.

From it, you will see that:
The C to the left of Middle C is called
'The C below Middle C'
The C to the right of Middle C is called
'The C above Middle C'

You should, at this stage, be able to find these
three C's right away.

Learn to find them this easy way:
• Play Middle C with the right hand
  (any finger will do).
• Play Middle C with the left hand.
• Play The C below Middle C with the left hand.
• Play The C above Middle C with the right hand.
• Finally: play Middle C again with one of
  the fingers of each hand.

*You now know where to find Middle C
and the C's immediately above and below it.*

How To Work Out Chords

With this easy-to-use guide you will be able to work out any major, minor, augmented and diminished chord on any note. Follow the simple formulae and all the chords you need will be at your fingertips.

Types Of Chord
Broadly speaking, there are four types of chord:

MAJOR (e.g. C)
MINOR (e.g. Cm)
DIMINISHED (e.g. C°)
AUGMENTED (e.g. C⁺)

MAJOR and MINOR are the two most important types: popular Western music is based on them. It is possible to play most popular tunes using MAJOR and MINOR chords only.

DIMINISHED and AUGMENTED are merely 'passing' or linking chords: they are used for passing from one Major or Minor chord to another.

Working Out Your Own Chords: Using Semitones
It is possible to work out any of the four types of chord by using simple formulae. These formulae rely on SEMITONES.

A SEMITONE is the smallest possible distance on a keyboard, counting black and white notes:-

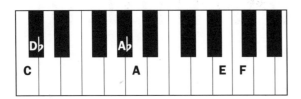

C to D♭ (or back) is the distance of ONE SEMITONE
A♭ to A (or back) is the distance of ONE SEMITONE
E to F (or back) is the distance of ONE SEMITONE

Chord Formulae
MAJOR 4-3 Semitones
MINOR 3-4 Semitones
DIMINISHED 3-3 Semitones
AUGMENTED 4-4 Semitones

Example 1
To find the chord of C (Major).
Formula: C-4-3

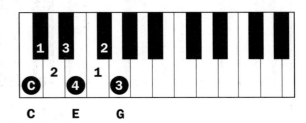

Play note C, then count 4 SEMITONES to the right, and you will arrive at the note E. Play note E, then count 3 SEMITONES to the right, and you will arrive at the note G. The notes of the chord are therefore: C, E, G.

Example 2
To find the chord of D♭ (Major).
Formula: D♭-4-3

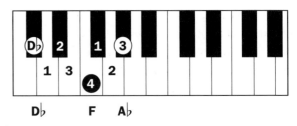

Play note D♭, then count 4 SEMITONES to the right, and you will arrive at the note F.
Play note F, then count 3 SEMITONES to the right, and you will arrive at the note A♭.
The notes of the chord are therefore: D♭, F, A♭.

Example 3
To find the chord of G (Minor).
Formula: G-3-4

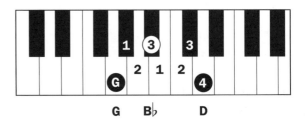

Play note G, then count 3 SEMITONES to the right, and you will arrive at the note B♭.
Play note B♭, then count 4 SEMITONES to the right, and you will arrive at the note D.
The notes of the chord are therefore: G, B♭, D.